MIRIAM DEFENSOR SANTIAGO
STUPID IS FOREVER
ABS-CBN
PUBLISHING

STUPID IS FOREVER

First Printing, December 2014
Second Printing, December 2014
Third Printing, December 2014
Fourth Printing, January 2015

Author Miriam Defensor Santiago

Publisher Alexie Renz M. Cruz
Research Assistants Marie Angelica Thelmo,
Jeanie Rose Bacong and Peter Tom Tolibas
Editorial Assistant Arlyn Rosales

Art Director Noel Avendaño
Cover Illustration Cj de Silva-Ong

President Ernesto L. Lopez
Managing Director Mark J. Yambot
Content Director Christina N. Lopez
Head, Special Projects Kristine V. Hernandez

Pre-Press Production Manager Andy Lizardo
Digital Imaging Supervisor Gil Cargason
Digital Artist Seb Cachola
Production Coordinator Jouie Doca
Purchasing Officer Arnel C. Bon

Head, Narrowcast and DTT Channels Antonio S. Ventosa
Sr. Finance Officer-Narrowcast Myca G. Ramos

ISBN 978-971-816-127-2

ABS-CBN
PUBLISHING INC.

PUBLISHED BY
ABS-CBN PUBLISHING, INC.
8F ELJCC Building
Mother Ignacia St., cor.
Eugenio Lopez Drive,
Quezon City, Philippines

The National Library of the Philippines CIP Data

Recommended entry:

      Santiago, Miriam Defensor.
          Stupid is Forever / Miriam Defensor Santiago.
      -- (Place of publication not identified) : ABS-CBN
      Publishing, Inc., [c2014]

          p.132 ; 17.18 cm

          ISBN 978-971-816-127-8

          1. Santiago, Miriam Defensor -- Humor.
      2. FIlipino wit and humor. 3. English wit and humor
      -- Philippines. 4. Speeches, lectures, etc., Filipino --
      Women authors. I. Title

      808.882 PN6222.P5 2014   P420140283

Dedicated to my sons
Archie and A.R.,
who traded bon mots with me everyday
at the dining table, until one day I
floored them with the question:
"Why is there something instead of
nothing?" In disgust, they chorused:
"That's not funny!" and walked out.

Foreword

Of course, I make no claim to originality in this compilation of my epigrams. My supporters find them funny, and my enemies presumably find them revolting. That's because those villains are hardwired only for self-adulation.

Anyway, I imbibed the responses in this volume from joke books, epigrammatic collections, magazines, the native intelligence of Filipino humor, and the need to survive the pomposity and superficiality of politicians, who wouldn't recognize sarcasm if it jumped up and bit them in the supercilious nose.

This work, commissioned by my publisher, serves as the second, enlarged edition of the well-received The Miriam Dictionary, which was circulated during the 1992 presidential campaign. This work is premised on my firm belief that despite what the bible implies, God definitely has a sense of humor.

MIRIAM DEFENSOR SANTIAGO
October 2014

About The Author

Sense of humor is almost absent among politicians, but Senator Miriam Defensor Santiago is a truly talented exception. People are puzzled how she can spontaneously make them laugh in the midst of national policy crises, and of real danger to her life as a corruption fighter.

Contrast adds to the humor, because Miriam is a leading Asian intellectual. She was elected judge of the International Criminal Court in December 2011, only to give it up because of cancer. Millions of her fans still believe she won but was cheated of the presidency in 1992. She lost one of only two beloved children. But she never lost her sense of humor.

Humor pushed Miriam the senator to help uncover the biggest corruption scandal in our country's political history. In dealing with the plunder of billions of public funds, and in standing by the rule of law in a highly politicized impeachment process, she scolded: "What the . . . . ?" later shortened to "Wha'?"

Miriam will go down in history not only as a laureate of the Magsaysay Award for government service, or as the candidate who never conceded defeat in a fraud-marred presidential election, but as the soul who rises above it all by laughing at human foibles.

Her complete resume can be found at the end of this book.

CONTENTS

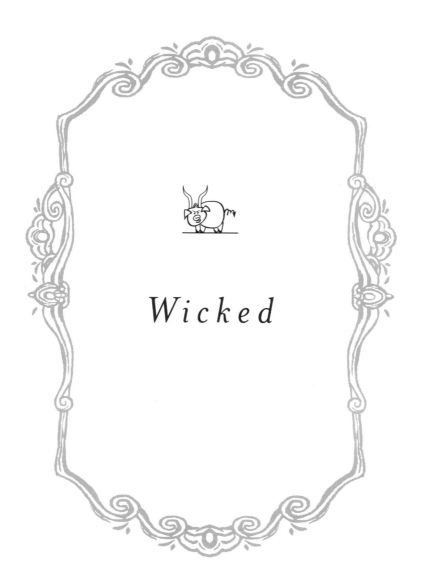

Wicked

His (Miriam's enemy) memory is in black and white.

———

He (Miriam's enemy) was a waiter at the Last Supper.

———

Politicians never get lost in thought,
because it's unfamiliar territory.

———

Brains aren't everything. In the case of
Congress members, they're nothing.

———

Corrupt politicians would be different, if
they had enough oxygen at birth.

———

Most people live and learn. Politicians just live.

———

In the Senate, sometimes I debate with people who
don't let the facts get in the way of their opinions,
as in the case of the Reproductive Health Bill.

I want to work as a judge of the International Criminal Court, because in Congress, the mediocrity of some people is unparalleled.

———

He (Filipino politician) is just not user-friendly.

———

To politicians accused of plunder: As an outsider, what do you think of the human race?

———

Of her enemy: Googling him yielded no results.

———

Of her pet peeve: He is so ugly he should donate his face to the Parks and Wildlife Office in Quezon City.

———

Like Voltaire, I believe that the ideal form of government is democracy tempered with assassination.

I don't mind dying for the Filipino youth and nation,
but I certainly don't want to die for politicians.

I agree with Mencken that democracy is a pathetic belief
in the collective wisdom of individual ignorance.

———

The speeches of young, ambitious, apparently
corrupt politicians leave the impression of an army of
pompous phrases moving over the political landscape
in search of an idea. Sometimes these meandering
words would actually capture a straggling thought
and bear it triumphantly as a prisoner in their
midst, until it died of servitude and overwork.
This is how I feel when I watch these talkative,
pompous and empty young people answer media
questions during a live TV interview.

———

On live TV interviews after a plenary session,
some Congress members look so blank, each one
of them looks like the guy in a science fiction
movie who is first to see the Creature.

———

Sometimes I meet my enemy in the Senate lounge
and would receive from him the sort of greetings
a corpse would give to an undertaker.

Many senators like to deliver speeches in the Senate — namely, privilege speeches, sponsorship speeches, speeches of commendation. They speak for hundreds of minutes and the visitors in the gallery are able to detect only one argument.

———

Someone working in the presidential staff in Malacañang loves to appear on TV, looking very much like a female llama surprised in her bath.

———

Celebrities who act as poster boys for stem cell treatment are bound to lose the temporary youthful look and then each one becomes a triumph of the embalmer's art.

———

On her Magsaysay Award for Government Service:
Bureaucracy is a giant mechanism operated by pygmies. Here are guidelines for bureaucrats:
When in charge, ponder.
When in trouble, delegate.
When in doubt, mumble.

Of the crime of plunder: Nothing is politically
right which is morally wrong.

———

Of the social event known as State of the Nation Address:
Some women wear too much makeup and
some women wear too little clothes.

———

A politician is a man who will double cross
that bridge when he comes to it.

———

As Galbraith said, there are times in politics
when you must be on the right side and lose.

———

Plato was so right: the price of apathy toward
public affairs is to be ruled by evil men.

———

In a corrupt country, if you want to succeed in politics,
you must keep your conscience under control.

———

The members of Congress are the people who
will support the President when he is wrong.

"You're the reason God created the middle finger."

A statesman is a politician who places himself at the service of the nation. A politician is a statesman who places the nation at his service. In the Philippines, another name for politician is plunder genius.

———

There are no true friends in politics. Someone said that we are all sharks circling, and waiting for traces of blood to appear in the water.

———

Of her political enemy always angling for a government job: If left out he would be dangerous, but if taken in, he would simply be destructive.

———

Of a wishy-washy politician: When in doubt on what should be done, his policy is to do nothing.

———

There are politicians who, when they were in power, were snobbish and arrogant. Now that these politicians have lost their jobs, there is nothing as abject and pathetic as they are. They remind me of a retired stud horse.

———

According to Mencken, the whole aim of practical politics is to keep the populace alarmed (and hence

clamorous to be led to safety) by menacing it with an
endless series of hobgoblins, all of them imaginary.

Ang pulitiko, para sumikat, ay tinatakot muna ang taong-
bayan na may malaking problema, kagaya ng kidnap for
ransom. Pagkatapos nagpapanggap na siya lang ang may
kakayahan na lumutas ng problema. Ang totoo, siya
pala ang may hawak ng mga kidnappers. Ang galing!

Some politicians get elected because they are well known.
The other politicians are defeated for the same reason.

In any Congress, out of 100 people, 2 are honest and
intelligent, 10 are criminals, and 88 are good for nothing.

Is there a good politician? Is there an honest burglar?

In any country, crooks make money by
underestimating the intelligence of the masses.

I sponsored and defended the Reproductive Health
Law, although I am a Catholic. In the Catholic church,
a woman to avoid pregnancy is allowed to resort to
mathematics. Thank God, now Catholic women
are allowed to resort to physics and chemistry!

———

Of her political enemy: He has all the characteristics
of an ambitious politician: a horrible voice,
bad breeding, and a vulgar manner.

———

During any commencement exercise, I always know
the graduate who will succeed. He is the person who
knows nothing and thinks he has everything. This
graduate will become a successful politician.

———

There was a time when a circus did not consist of
trained animal performers and acrobatic shows, but
of freaks and monstrosities. One of them was called
"the boneless wonder." They are now in politics.

I'm so jealous that you finally found your true love.
Unfortunately, they haven't legalized self-marriage yet.

People are entitled to change their minds. But when politicians do so, they always explain it in terms of incomprehensible principles.

———

In Philippine politics, I know many men and women who are able to rise above principles.

———

When I listen to the defensive language of those accused of plunder, I marvel that they can make lies sound truthful, plunder respectable, and give an appearance of solidity to pure wind.

———

When people say that politics is the art of the possible, they mean the art of speculation, calculation, intrigue, secret deals, and pragmatic maneuvering.

———

Members of Congress are eager to participate and be televised during public hearings, which are more like police investigations conducted by a scatterbrained investigator. The honorable men and women of Congress like to take things apart. Unfortunately, they have no clue on how to put them back together.

Let me quote the epigram that the purification
of politics is an iridescent dream.

———

Every time the President fills a vacant office, he
makes a hundred malcontents and one ingrate.

———

Democracy is a wonderful system. It permits
you to vote for a politician, and then to watch
on TV as he is tried for plunder and graft.

———

The people charged with plunder have
a sickness called spendicitis.

———

Many politicians refuse to answer media questions,
on the ground that it might eliminate them.
I try to give the politicians in the Senate facts,
and then they draw their own confusions.

The Napoles scandal showed that some politicians are the same all over the country. They promise to build bridges where there are no rivers.

———

When you watch every politician answer questions from the media, you realize that a politician approaches every subject with an open mouth.

———

I know a politician who is so windy that he can give mouth-to-mouth resuscitation by telephone.

———

The trouble with my enemies is that too many of them received an honorary degree from an elementary school.

———

Politicians are fond of saying "we." The only people entitled to use "we" are monarchs, editorial writers, and pregnant women.

"Let's switch places: you be funny and I'll be an asshole."

In spite of its great accomplishments in modern times, science has not yet discovered adequate controls for a number of national phenomena, including climate change, storm surge, tsunamis, and politicians.

———

Darwin's theory of evolution suggests that first came the baboon, and then man. Politics proves that Darwin is wrong, and that first came man, and then the baboon.

———

A political candidate once said that he would rather be right than be president. But the Constitution provides that you can be both.

———

As Theodore Roosevelt said, the most practical kind of politics is the politics of decency.

———

Two political candidates were engaged in a heated debate:
Candidate 1: What about the powerful interests that control you?
Candidate 2: You leave my wife out of this!

I love this definition from Ambrose Bierce. A politician is an eel in the fundamental mud, upon which the superstructure of organized society is reared. When he wriggles, he mistakes the agitation of his tail for the trembling of the edifice. As compared with the statesman, he suffers the disadvantage of being alive.

———

To call a Filipino politician a mediocre man is unwanted flattery. Many politicians are men of monumental littleness.

———

All professionals in our country need to pass a government exam. Only a politician does not need any kind of preparation to practice.

PSALM OF THE POLITICIAN

The politician is my shepherd, I'm in want,
He makes me to lie down on park benches
He leads me beside the still factories.
He disturbs my soul.
Yes, though I walk through the valley of the shadow
of depression and recession,
I anticipate no recovery, for he is with me.
He prepares a reduction in my salary in the presence
of my enemies,
He anointed my small income with great losses.
My expenses alarmingly run over.
Surely unemployment and poverty shall follow me all
the days of my life
And I shall dwell in a mortgaged home forever.

Asukal Ka,
Ako Ay Sago

Ang pag-ibig natin ay parang Facebook. Pwedeng i-like, pwede ring mag-comment, pero hindi dapat i-share.

———

Ang crush parang math problem, kung hindi mo makuha, titigan mo na lang.

———

Pumupunta ka ba sa gym? Kasi feeling ko, magwo-work out tayo.

———

Ang pagmamahal ko sa'yo ay parang bilbil, pilit ko mang tinatago pero halata pa rin!

———

Hindi ako mataba. Hindi lang ako madaling ma-kidnap.

———

Kung isa akong joke, gusto ko 'yung mapipikon ka, para naman seryosohin mo ako.

———

Wow, saan gawa ang t-shirt mo? Gawa ba 'yan sa boyfriend material?

Ang pag-ibig ko sa'yo ay parang relo.
Parating pakanan, never kakaliwa.

———

Ang ganda mo ay parang PLDT—pang-long distance.

———

Kung magkaroon man ako ng third eye, ilalagay ko ito
sa puso ko. Para hindi na ako mabulag sa pag-ibig.

———

Alam niyo ba kung kailan nauso ang pick-up
lines? Noong pumasok ako sa UP College of Law,
naglabasan na ang mga pick-up lines. Noong mga
panahon ding iyon nakita ako ng mga lalaking may
girlfriend na, kaya nauso rin ang BREAK-UP.

———

Kapag namatay na ako, huwag na huwag kang pupunta
sa libingan ko, baka tumibok ulit ang puso ko.

———

Miss, kutsara ka ba? Kasi papalapit ka
pa lang, napapanganga na ako.

Kung asukal ka, ako naman ay sago.
Wala akong kwenta kung wala ang tamis mo.

Suicide. Homicide. Insecticide. Lahat
na lang pamatay. Pero kung gusto mo ng
pampabuhay, i-try mo ang "by my side."

Malabo na talaga ang mga mata ko. Pwede ba akong
humingi sa iyo ng kahit konting pagtingin?

Laway ka ba? Kasi kahit tulog na ako, ikaw
pa rin ang lumalabas sa bibig ko.

Ang lampa mo naman! Tatawid ka na nga lang
sa isip ko, nahulog ka pa sa puso ko.

Sabi nila, "A picture is worth a thousand words."
Pero nang nakita ko ang picture mo, tatlong
words lang ang naisip ko: "I love you."

Password ka ba? Hindi kasi kita kayang
kalimutan, pero kaya kitang palitan.

Tinanong minsan ni Boy si Girl:
BOY: Anong tunog ng aso?
GIRL: Aww aww.
BOY: Eh ang pusa?
GIRL: Eh di meow meow.
BOY: Eh ang puso ko?
GIRL: Ano?
BOY: Ikaw ikaw.

———

Hindi naman tayo naglalaro ng tagu-taguan
pero bakit hinahanap-hanap kita?

———

Mag-exchange gift tayo? Akin ka at sa iyo naman ako.

———

Pwede ba kitang sabayan pauwi? Kasi sabi sa akin
ng magulang ko, "Follow your dreams."

———

Test paper ka ba? Nauubos na kasi oras ko kakatitig
sa'yo, ayan tuloy babagsak na yata ako sa'yo!

Dilim ka ba? Kasi nang dumating ka,
wala na akong makitang iba.

———

Alam mo ba, ang bigas, gasolina, pamasahe,
tuition fee, isda, karne, lahat sila nagmamahalan?
Tayo na lang kaya ang hindi!

———

Pangalan mo palang kinikilig na ako, paano
kaya kung magka-apelyido na tayo?

———

Ok lang akong mahilo, basta sa iyo
lang iikot ang mundo ko.

———

Dalawang beses lang naman kita gustong
makasama: now and forever.

———

Dahil isa akong judge, pwede kitang hatulan ng
habang buhay na pagkakakulong sa puso ko.

Kung ang mga bagay ay makapagsasalita:

"You never know what you have until you lose it, and once you lose it, you can never get it back." — *Snatcher*

"Ginawa ko naman lahat para sumaya ka. Mahirap ba talagang makuntento sa isa? Bakit palipat-lipat ka?" — *TV*

"Kapag nagmamahal ako lagi na lang maraming tao ang nagagalit! Wala ba akong karapatang magmahal?!" — *Gasoline*

"Pinapaikot mo lang ako. Nagsasawa na ako. Mabuti pang patayin mo na lang ako." — *Electric fan*

"Hindi lahat ng maasim may vitamin C." — *Kili-kili*

"Hindi lahat ng bumabakat sa damit ay nakakaakit." — *Bilbil*

———

Can you recommend a good bank? Kasi I'm planning to save all my love for you.

Hirit ng mag-boyfriend:

Boy: Para kang pangalan ko.
Girl: Bakit naman?
Boy: 'Pag nawala ka, sino ako?

———

Girl: Saan tayo magde-date sa Valentines Day?
Boy: Sa sementeryo?
Boy: Bakit 'dun?
Boy: Para mapatunayan kong patay na patay ako sayo.
At pumunta nga sina Boy and Girl sa
sementeryo para mag-ghost hunting. Habang
naglalakad sila sa pinakamadilim na bahagi ng
sementeryo, biglang napasigaw si Boy.
BOY: Naku! Hala! Naramdaman mo ba 'yun?!
GIRL: Alin?!
BOY: Na mahal kita.

———

Pedicab ka ba?
PEDICABang i-date sa Valentines Day?

———

Ang pag-ibig ko sa'yo ay parang LANGKA.
LANGKAtupasan.

35

Kili-kili ka ba?
Malapit ka kasi sa puso ko.

———

Ang love ay parang bayad sa jeep.
Minsan hindi nasusuklian.

———

Ang sabi nila "An apple a day keeps the doctor away."
Kung guwapo o maganda ang doctor, ayoko na ng apple.

———

Pwede bang magpa-blood test? Para
malaman mo na type kita.

———

Gusto kitang kasuhan ng trespassing. Basta-
basta ka na lang pumapasok sa puso ko.

———

Empleyado ka ba? Empleyado rin ako.
Pwede tayong magkaroon ng union.

Ang relasyon ay parang gubat. Madalas may ahas.

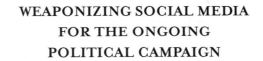

WEAPONIZING SOCIAL MEDIA FOR THE ONGOING POLITICAL CAMPAIGN

By

SENATOR MIRIAM DEFENSOR SANTIAGO

(Excerpt from the speech delivered at the UP Manila on 12 February 2013,
at the symposium sponsored by the University Student Council)

WEAPONIZING SOCIAL MEDIA

The campaign period has begun. All kinds of characters want to run for public office. We, the 52 million Filipino voters, are bored with their antics. We are aghast at their resumes. Some of them are not even high school graduates. They resort to all kinds of cheap gimmickry, hoping to provide entertainment for free. They should not be called candidates; they should be called clowns.

In the Philippines, politics is dominated by two kinds of clowns: rich clowns; and poor clowns hoping to become rich. Fortunately, we are at the cusp of a new ominous wave of change in the political beach. This wave is called the social media. In the Philippines, nobody knows how to control or manage social media. Rich clowns used to bribe press and broadcast journalists so that they could gain added illegal advantage over their competitors. But now, the rich clowns are beginning to discover that it is not possible to bribe the leaders, much less, all the netizens in cyberspace.

If the first Edsa revolution was a "Xerox revolution", and if Edsa 2 was a "text revolution", then the next revolution against political corruption should be called the "Net revolution".

The ideal UP student always gives the world a shock. I ask each one of you to give the mindless political candidates a shock, by demoting TV, which used to be the king of political advertising, and instead elevating as political campaign weapons the tablet and the smart phone.

In terms of social network use, the Philippines is ranked among the top countries. This could be the precursor of the participatory democracy of the future. Facebook is the premier social media service in the world. Twitter is an online social networking and micro-blogging service. YouTube provides a forum for the distribution of video content, particularly eyewitness features of political protests. Facebook, Twitter, and YouTube are the so-called big three social media services. These services enable large numbers of people to be easily and inexpensively contacted via a variety of services.

Social media lowers traditional socio-economic barriers to commanding the spotlight. The power of the rich politicians becomes more porous and the political warlords have less control. It has been said that text messaging, Facebook, Twitter, YouTube, and the Internet have given rise to a reservoir of political energy. Digital technologies enforce the formation and activities of civil society groups: mobs, movements, and civil society organizations.

CHALLENGE TO UP STUDENTS

The ideal UP student is not interesting per se. What is interesting is what the ideal student does with his life after graduation from UP. As a rule, any UP graduate will always be characterized by academic excellence and by the courage to take social justice to the next level. If you are to serve your nation, I am here to testify that it will be a rough, contentious, and spirit-crushing journey.

But as a true UP graduate, I insist that I have a role to perform. This role is to stand as one of gazillion bricks in the cathedral of governance. No one will remember me if I suddenly drop dead tomorrow. But generations after you and me, would be able to put behind them the culture of corruption, and build a new shining nation with leaders who are neither dazzled by the material world, nor confused about their purpose in life.

Hence, I have risen from my sickbed to issue you this challenge: For God's sake, save this country. Use social media during this three-month campaign period to ensure that our people shall be led to choose deserving national leaders. Allow me to make some recommendations on how to weaponize social media against the corrupt, the clueless, and the clowns. I am paraphrasing from an article in the Net issued by Craft Media Digital and written by Brian Donahue.

Weaponize social media during the campaign by providing content that not only informs, but also entertains and motivates. You need to develop skills in creative design, emotionally riveting visuals, and content that inspires action. We can not weaponize by simply issuing a statement, a newsletter, or a Facebook post. We need to enlist the work of more graphic designers, creative writers, videographers, and musicians.

Weaponize social media during the campaign by embracing targeted messaging strategies. You cannot rely on single-issue national messaging. You have to send custom messages to specific audiences online. It is said that in today's digital age, data is the most precious commodity. Hook up with math students in the Diliman campus. Ask our math scholars to build algorithms for matching data. This will develop demographic models that will help you to identify valuable voter behavior. For example, refer to Facebook OpenGraph.

Weaponize social media during the political campaign by delivering content so engaging that individual netizens will be motivated to share it. I see in the current campaign that the most egregious error of the candidates is that they treat social media as if it were TV or radio, where they simply transfer information to the masses. The strength of the web is information sharing among social netizens.

Weaponize social media in the political campaign by accepting that the future of political warfare will take place online. For example, a comparative database that provides information on each candidate's age, residence, highest academic degree, and highest professional achievement, would be a sufficient counterbalance to the tendency of the low middle-class voter to sell his vote or to vote for the cute personality.

Social media should be used as a showcase for intangible movement or energy, and a medium of information to motivate people to vote for or against a particular candidate.

Conclusion

I share one unbreakable linkage with you. At one time I was your age and like all UP students, I wanted to change the world. Maybe I have. But the world also changed me. Now I am old enough to have seen the world and have all my illusions shattered. Am I disillusioned? No, because as the poet said:

Though much is taken, much abides;
and though
We are not now that strength which in old days
Moved earth and heaven, that which we are,
we are;
One equal temper of heroic hearts,
Made weak by time and fate, but strong in will
To strive, to seek, to find, and not to yield.

Death Threats
for
Breakfast!

Barring public demand, any person who pursues
the presidency out of personal ambition must
be suffering from a basic genetic defect.
(In a 1989 magazine interview.)

———

I do not subscribe to the school of thought that I am
leading the presidential polls because of my beautiful legs.
(After topping most presidential surveys in 1990.)

———

First you say that I have a brilliant resume and an
impressive track record. But then you propose that
I should not run for president, but only for vice-
president. Clearly, your conclusion does not follow
your own premise. And you justify this illogic
by claiming that I would be cheated by my rivals
as a presidential candidate, so I should settle for
becoming a vice-presidential candidate instead.
Sir, if the rest of humankind had adopted your
line of thinking, we would never have reached the
moon, scaled Mt. Everest, or learned to fly. For
in all these daring enterprises, people who should
have known better said it could not be done.
When I went to the Commission on Immigration
and Deportation to fight graft and corruption, the
cynics also said it could not be done. But a person's
reach must exceed her grasp, or what's heaven for?

Why did Sir Edmund Hillary climb Mt.
Everest? Because it is there. Why am I fighting
graft and corruption? Because it is here!
That's why I'm running for president,
and for no other post.
*(During an open forum hosted by the Association of International
College Women, who gave her a standing ovation.)*

Sir, I remind you that as the Commissioner of
Immigration and Deportation, I represent the
majesty of the Republic of the Philippines. You
have the obligation to show respect and courtesy to
me. Now shut up, or I'll knock your teeth off!
*(To an alien criminal suspect who raised his voice to
interrupt her during a press conference.)*

The fixer is a person who nominally looks like a
human being. But he specializes in creating misery for
others, in order that he can offer to fix it for a fee.
*(Explaining to the press why she banned fixers at Commission on
Immigration and Deportation and ordered their mass arrest.)*

Ano ang pinagkapareho ng sperm at ng mga pulitiko?
Pareho silang may one in a million chance na maging totoong tao.

The cabinet is afflicted with a dreaded disease. It is known as logorrhea, or incoherent talking.
(After then President Corazon Aquino announced a program of measures to improve cabinet performance and cut costs, most of which had been proposed earlier by Miriam.)

———

Congress and the cabinet are talking at cross-purposes. We are trapped in a political Tower of Babel. Our national leaders are accursed by glossolalia, or talking in different tongues.
(When the Senate first began to oppose her alien legalization program when she was Immigration Commissioner.)

———

I shall expect the landlords to cooperate with the agrarian reform program. Right now, it looks like I'm headed for One Hundred Years of Solitude.
(Upon President Aquino's announcement of her appointment as Secretary of Agrarian Reform, using the title of a book by Nobel prizewinner Gabriel Garcia Marquez.)

———

Some of them are devotees to a cult of self-praise. I refused to join that hallelujah chorus!
(To a newsman's question of why some of her cabinet colleagues accused her of aloofness when she was Secretary of Agrarian Reform.)

I feel like Indiana Jones in the Temple of Doom.
*(Entering Congress for her first confirmation
hearing as Secretary of Agrarian Reform.)*

———◦———

I was accused of almost every crime under the Penal Code,
except adultery. At malapit na rin kaming dumating doon.
(Explaining why confirmations hearings could be oppressive.)

———◦———

Head-bashing is the best strategy. Sometimes I
have to splatter their brains on the pavement.
(On the best way to fight graft.)

———◦———

When the government employee is poor and he works in a
corrupt agency, he can resist everything except temptation.
(At a student convocation at the University of the Philippines.)

———◦———

I don't mind if a senator does not know much about
legislative work, what I mind is when they pretend they
do! They reduce legislation to the level of the ludicrous.

Holdaper: Holdap ito! Akin na ang pera mo!
Lalaki: Hindi mo ba ako nakikilala?
Isa akong congressman!
Holdaper: Kung ganoon, akin na ang pera namin!

———

My public life closely resembles the popular science-
fiction trilogy on screen, consisting of the movies
entitled "Star Wars," followed by "The Empire Strikes
Back," and ending with "The Return of the Jedi."
In seeking to change the culture of corruption, I have to
fight willy-nilly the superstars of the political underworld
in this country. Although I am a definite underdog, I
am not afraid of those corrupt superstars. Thus, the
first chapter of my life should be entitled "Star Wars."
Because I was able to conscienticize the public about
corrupt politics, my enemies sought to avenge themselves.
They refused to confirm me in the Commission
on Appointments, until I was removed from the
Cabinet. My enemies posted that evil victory, but
until now they do not stop. When I started leading the
presidential surveys, they paid for a diabolic media
blitz against me. Thus, the second chapter of my life
should be entitled "The Empire Strikes Back."
But we have not seen the end of this trilogy. For life,
like theology, consists of the unceasing battle between
good and evil. In the movie trilogy, the forces of
good were called Jedi, while the forces of evil were

I eat death threats for breakfast!

called the Empire. I have no doubt that, in the end,
the forces of evil in Philippine politics will triumph.
Thus, I promise you, the third chapter of our life
together shall be entitled "The Return of the Jedi."
*(From a speech at the St. Louis University gymnasium in Baguio
City, where over 5,000 students gave her a standing ovation,
presaging her phenomenally popular campus tour of the country,
and prompting media to call her "the new campus heroine.")*

The only thing we are not importing is our politicians
because that is what we have in abundance.

A person suffering from lung cancer is
prone to bleeding. I used to have high pain
tolerance, that's why I'm in politics.

How to tell if a politician is telling the truth:
Whenever he's crossing his arms, he
might be telling the truth.
Whenever he's stroking his chin, he
might be telling the truth.
Whenever he looks at you straight in the
eye, he might be telling the truth.
But when he opens his mouth, he is lying.

Corrupt politician, nagyayabang: Ako ang tumulong
sa mga businessmen na maging milyonaryo!
Miriam: Bakit, ano ba sila dati?
Corrupt politician: Bilyonaryo.

———

I have realized why corrupt politicians do nothing
to improve the quality of public school education.
They are terrified of educated voters.

———

Ang sabi ng gobyerno: Don't lie. Don't cheat.
Don't steal. Don't sell drugs. Don't kill.
Alam ninyo kung bakit? Ayaw ng
gobyerno ng competition.

———

Hindi ba, ang mga gadget kapag nagloko,
namamatay? Dapat ganyan din ang mga
pulitikong manloloko, namamatay din!

———

Question: Ano ang resulta ng IQ exam
ng mga kurakot na pulitiko?
Answer: Negative.

What is the difference between corruption in the
U.S. and corruption in the Philippines?
Answer: In the U.S. they go to jail. In the
Philippines, they go to the U.S.

———

Corrupt official: Miriam, kapag natapos
ang term ko, iiyak ka ba?
Miriam : Oo naman. Mapipigilan ko ba ang tears of joy?

———

Pulitiko ka ba? Ang ganda kasi ng mga
mata mo. Corrupt nang corrupt.

———

May mga kandidatong guilty ng trespassing.
Kumbaga sa college grades, ang nakuha
lang nila ay "tres" na passing grade.

———

MGA ONLINE ACTIVITIES NA DAPAT
ITURING NA CYBERCRIME:

Wrong grammar.
Premature campaigning ng mga epal politicians.
Photo albums na panay mukha mo lang ang
laman. Hindi porke bago ang hair-do mo,
magpopost ka na ng 100 pictures ng sarili mo.

"I do not subscribe to the school of thought that I am leading the presidential polls because of my beautiful legs."

Pwede bang kasuhan ng cybercrime ang kaaway mo tuwing magpo-post siya ng bagong profile picture? Nakaka-offend kasi. Ilegal dapat ang pagmumukha niya.

———

Bakit naka-schedule sa tag-init ang
kampanya para sa eleksyon?
Dahil dito napapatunayan kung anong
klaseng pulitiko ang nangangampanya.
Kung matunaw sila sa init, ibig sabihin plastic sila.
Kung masunog sila sa araw, ibig sabihin mapapel sila.
Kung mahilig silang magbilad sa
araw, malamang buwaya sila.

———

Nagkaroon ng pagkakataon na magtanong
ng tig-isang tanong kay God ang mga
presidente ng China, USA, at Pilipinas.
Nauna ang presidente ng China. Ang tanong
niya: "God, kailan po mawawala sa bansa
ko ang kurapsyon at kahirapan?"
Sumagot si God: "300 years, anak."
Umiyak ang presidente ng China: "Patay
na ako bago mangyari iyon!"
Sumunod ang presidente ng USA. Ang
tanong niya: "God, kailan po mawawala sa
bansa ko ang kurapsyon at kahirapan?"
Sumagot si God: "500 years, anak."

Umiyak ang presidente ng USA: "Patay
na ako bago mangyari iyon!"
Sumunod ang presidente ng Pilipinas. Ang
tanong niya: "God, kailan po mawawala sa
bansa ko ang kurapsyon at kahirapan?"
Umiyak si God. Sabi niya: "Patay tayo diyan."

———

Kapag nagsinungaling ka sa congressman o sa
senador, kakasuhan ka na ng perjury, may jail
term ka pa. Pero kapag ang congressman o senador
nagsinungaling sa iyo, ginagawa lang nila ang trabaho
nila, magkakaroon pa sila ng bagong term.

———

Ano ang tawag kapag nagtapon ka ng basura sa dagat?
Sagot: Pollution.
Ano naman ang tawag kapag tinapon mo sa
dagat ang mga pulitikong kurakot?
Sagot: Solution.

———

Kapag hindi nanalo ang ine-endorso kong kandidato,
para itong kape na walang creamer at asukal. Napakapait.

There was a study on the connection between
government employees and the sport they play.
Ang paboritong sport daw ng mga entry-level
na government employees ay basketball.
Kapag lower management position,
paborito daw nila ay bowling.
Kapag upper management naman,
paborito daw nila ay tennis.
Ang paborito daw na sport ng mga high-
level government officials ay golf.
The study then made this conclusion: Kapag tumataas
ang posisyon mo sa gobyerno, lumiliit ang iyong balls.

Top three na pinakasinungaling na trabaho sa Pilipinas:
3. Beautician. Sasabihin nilang maganda ang
customer kahit hindi naman talaga.
2. Kundoktor ng jeep. Sasabihin nila na
dalawa pa ang kasya kahit puno na.
1. Pulitiko.

Dahil puno na ng kasamaan ang mundo, pinuntahan
ng Diyos si Noah, na ngayon ay nakatira sa Pilipinas.
Inutos sa kanya ng Diyos: "Gumawa ka ulit ng isang arko,
ilagay mo dito ang dalawang pares ng bawat hayop sa

mundo. Pagkatapos ng anim na buwan, uulan at babaha
ng apatnapung araw at gugunawin ko ang mundo."
Pagkalipas ng anim na buwan, binalikan ng Diyos
si Noah. Nakita niya na walang arko si Noah.
Sabi ni Noah, "Pasensya na, Lord. Hindi ko po
natapos ang arko. Iba na po ang panahon ngayon:
Una, kailangan ko raw po ng building permit.
Sunod, nahirapan po akong makakuha ng
kahoy na hindi galing sa illegal logging.
Mahal po ang kuryente panggawa ng arko, hindi
po ako makakuha ng discount sa Meralco.
Nahirapan po akong makakuha ng environmental permit
sa DENR dahil sa mga endangered species na dadalhin ko.
Ayaw po maniwala sa akin ng PAGASA na may dadating na
malakas na ulan at baha dahil luma na ang equipment nila.
Pinapa-lifestyle check po ako ng BIR,
dapat daw magbayad ako ng buwis.
Hindi rin po ako makakuha ng funding sa
Congress, hindi raw nila gusto yung NGO ko.
Patawad po, Lord. Hindi ko po natapos
ang arko sa loob ng anim na buwan."
Sumagot si Lord: "Hindi ko na gugunawin ang
mundo. Naunahan na ako ng gobyerno."

There's still a double standard.
The place where a woman sells herself is called
a house of ill-repute or a brothel.
The place where a man sells himself is
called the House of Representatives.

———

Ano ang pinagkaiba ng holdaper sa pulitiko? Ang
holdaper magnanakaw muna bago tatakbo. Ang
pulitiko tatakbo muna bago magnanakaw.

———

One of these corrupt politicians went for a job
interview and the recruitment manager said: "We're
looking for someone who is responsible."
"Well, I'm your man for the job!" replied the
politician. "In my last job whenever everything
went wrong, they always said I was responsible."

Sabi ng isang survey, 25 percent ng mga pulitiko daw ay umiinom ng medication para sa kanilang mental illness. Malaking problema ito. Ibig sabihin 75 percent ay hindi umiinom ng gamot.

———

May isang pulitiko na lumapit sa isang psychiatrist. Ang sabi niya: "Doc, tulungan mo po ako. Tuwing nakakatanggap po ako ng pork barrel, hindi ko mapigilan ang sarili ko na nakawin ito. Nagi-guilty po ako at nade-depress nang malala at matagal dahil dito." Ang sabi ng psychiatrist: "Sige, tutulungan kitang magkaroon ng self-control para hindi ka na magnakaw sa taumbayan." Sumagot ang pulitiko: "Dok, huwag po! Gusto kong tulungan ninyo ako para hindi na ako ma-guilty at ma-depress."

———

Isang araw ng Linggo, nagsimba ang isang corrupt politician. Sabi ng pari sa kanyang sermon, "Magbigay ka sa simbahan ng ayon sa kabutihan ng iyong loob." Nang narinig iyon ng pulitiko, nagdonate siya ng 100 pesos. Nakita ito ng pari. Tinawag ng pari ang

I received a text message that said: Dear Miriam, Don't vote for Joker.
He's our enemy. Love, Batman and Robin

pulitiko. "Ano po iyon, Father?" tanong ng pulitiko.
Ang sabi ng pari, "ito ang sukli mo, 99 pesos."

———

What we are seeing is an epidemic of people in high
government office who possess the epidermis of
pachyderms and intestinal fortitude of anacondas.
(*On recent corruption scandals in government.*)

———

May tatlong doktor, pinag-uusapan kung anong
pasyente ang pinakamadaling operahan.
Sabi ng una: "Electricians! Everything
inside them is color-coded."
Sabi ng pangalawang doktor: "Librarians! Everything
inside them is in alphabetical order."
Sabi ng pangatlo: "Pulitiko ang pinakamadali! They
have no brains, no guts, no hearts, and no balls."

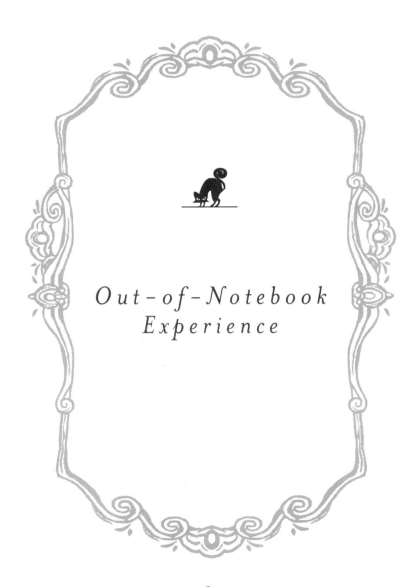

Out-of-Notebook Experience

The purpose of a teacher is to teach,
not teaching to flunk a class.

———

The paradigmatic teacher is one who
inspires you to read on your own.

———

Question: Anong sinabi ni Papaya nu'ng
tumingin sa kanya si Pineapple?
Answer: Oy ikaw, anong tinitingin, tingin,
tingin, tingin, tingin, tingin mo diyan?

———

Good news: Wala ka nang pimples!
Bad news: Dahil wala nang space.

———

Question: Do you know what the word "floral" means?
Answer: "Floral" is the opposite of "singular."

———

Question: What is the singular form
of the word "binoculars"?
Answer: Telescope.

Question: What is the plural form of iced tea?
Answer: Bottomless iced tea.

———

Question: What is the plural form of rice?
Answer: Extra rice.

———

Paano mo sasabihin sa kausap mo na maitim ang
kili-kili niya nang hindi siya magagalit?
Ganito: Ano ba ang ginagamit mong
deodorant, Kiwi shoe polish?

———

Hindi lahat ng sweet ay loyal sa'yo.
Tandaan, sweet nga ang candy, pero
nakabalot naman sa plastic.

———

Question: Paano mo sasabihin sa isang babae
na mataba siya na hindi siya mababastos?
Answer: Excuse me miss, Mang Tomas ba ang lotion mo?

———

Ang homework ay parang panliligaw. Sa bahay
dapat ginagawa, hindi sa paaralan.

Law school is quite easy. It's like a stroll in a park. Pero Jurassic Park.

Do you want a job where you get to travel a lot
and have lots of money in your hands?
Pwede kang konduktor ng bus.

———

Condolence nga pala…
Sa mga taong patay na patay sa akin.

———

Alam niyo ba kung bakit laging busy
ang magaganda at mga guwapo?
Explain ko sa inyo mamaya. Busy pa ako e.

———

Pedro: Gusto kong maging nurse
para makatulong sa kapwa.
Jose: Ako, gusto kong maging doktor,
para makapanggamot ng kapwa.
Kiko: Ako mayor, para mapagsilbihan ko ang kapwa ko.
Maria: Gusto kong maging presidente para
mapaglingkuran ko ang aking kapwa.
Juan Tamad: Ako naman, gusto kong maging kapwa.

Teacher: Class, anong gusto niyong maging paglaki niyo?
Juan: Gusto kong maging piloto.
Nena: Gusto kong maging teacher.
Maria: Gusto kong maging mabuting ina.
Pedro: Gusto kong gawing ina si Maria.

———

A true teacher does not terrorize ignorant
students, because a true teacher knows
that it is his job to cure ignorance.

———

Alam niyo ba ang alamat ng baboy? Minsan sa
sobrang galit ko, sinuntok ko sa ilong ang isang
elepante. Hindi na lumaki ang mga anak nya. Sa
kanya nag-umpisa ang kauna-unahang baboy.

———

Student: Ma'am, kamusta po ang grades ko?
Professor : Aba, iha, kasing-ganda ng buhok mo!
Parang bagong rebond. Bagsak na bagksak!

POLITICAL CORRECTNESS FOR TEENAGE STUDENTS:

No one fails a class anymore; they're
merely "passing impaired."
You don't have detention; you're just
one of the "exit delayed."
Your bedroom isn't cluttered; it's
just "passage restrictive."
These days, a student isn't lazy; he's
"energetically declined."
Your locker isn't overflowing with junk;
it's just "closure prohibitive."
Kids don't get grounded anymore; they
merely hit "social speedbumps."
Your homework isn't missing; it's just having
an "out-of-notebook experience."
You're not sleeping in class; you're
"rationing consciousness."
You're not late; you just have a "rescheduled arrival time."

Paano mo sasabihin sa kausap mong babae na mukha
siyang lalaki nang hindi siya masasaktan?
Ganito: Uy ang kyut-kyut mo naman! Kamukhang-
kamukha ka ng daddy mo!

WHAT NOT TO SAY AS A TEACHER:

Sa isang examination

Student: Ma'am, puwedeng gumamit ng liquid paper?
Teacher: Ang kulit naman! Sinabi
nang pad paper lang eh.

Pagkatapos ng examination

Teacher: Okay, time is up. One, two,
three. Come your papers to me!

Pagkatapos ng klase

Teacher to students: Okay class, it's time to go
home. Form a line and pass out slowly.

WRONG WORD USAGES

Laity – Hometown ni Imelda Marcos ang laity.
Mention – Ang laki ng bahay nila, parang mention.
Punctuation – Sabi ng isang bata,
"Daddy, pasukan na next week.

Kailangan ko po ng punctuation."
Tenacious – Before playing tennis I
have to put on my tenacious.
Curtain and Kitchen – Aray! Huwag
mo kong curtain. Masa-kitchen.

Subukan natin ang talino ninyo. Use the word
"ANYONE" in a sentence. Answer: "Nasaan
na kayo? Bakit niyo ako ANYONE?"

I heard one of the questions in the last bar exams
went like this: Should Santa Claus be considered a
criminal? The answer is yes. He is liable for crimes
such as illegal surveillance, unfair labor practices,
animal abuse, and breaking and entering.

Law school is quite easy. It's like a stroll
in a park. Pero Jurassic Park.

Ano ang sabi ng anak na caterpillar sa tatay caterpillar?
"'Tay, bilhan mo ako ng sapatos!"
Sumagot ang tatay caterpillar:
"Sipain kita d'yan e!"

Paano mo sasabihin sa classmate mo na bungi-
bungi ang ngipin niya nang hindi siya magagalit?
Ganito: Wow, classmate, ang ganda naman ng ngipin
mo! Para silang nag-eexam, one seat apart!

Boss: Why do you think we should hire you?
John: Kasi po bago pa lang po ako
kaya wala pa po akong sungay.
Boss: In English, please.
John: Ah, uhm, well you see I'm brand
new so I'm not yet horny.

Teacher: Use the word "beautiful" in a sentence.
Student: "My teacher is beautiful, isn't she?"
Teacher: Thank you, it's very flattering.
Now, translate it in Tagalog.
Student: "Ang guro ko ay maganda, maganda nga ba?"

Cardo: Pedro, nahirapan ka ba sa questions sa exam?
Pedro: Hindi naman!
Cardo: Ang galing mo naman!
Pedro: Nahirapan ako sa answers!

Teacher: Ano ang similarity nina Jose Rizal,
Andres Bonifacio, at Ninoy Aquino?
Student: Lahat sila, namatay ng holiday!

———

Madaling magkasakit ang mga sexy; ang mga crush
ng bayan; ang ma-appeal at henyo; ang kind,
thoughtful, smart, sweet, and malakas ang karisma.
Bigla yatang sumama ng pakiramdam ko, ah.

———

Hindi lahat ng nananalo ay magagaling
dahil may nandadaya.
Hindi lahat ng matalino ay mataas ang
grades dahil may nangongopya.
Hindi lahat ng artista ay sexy dahil di
naman ako artista, sexy lang talaga.

———

Gaano katalino ang estudyanteng Pilipino?
Common sense pa lang nila, IQ na ng ibang senator.

Alam niyo ba ang alamat ng giraffe? Minsan sa sobrang galit ko, binigyan ko ng uppercut ang isang kabayo. Sa kanya nag–umpisa ang kauna–unahang giraffe.

STUDENT LEADERSHIP

By

SENATOR MIRIAM DEFENSOR SANTIAGO

(Guest speaker at the awards convocation of the Lyceum of the
Philippines University, Batangas City, on 7 March 2014)

Ladies and gentlemen:

I am happy, despite my chronic fatigue syndrome, to come to this campus of the Lyceum of the Philippines University at Batangas City. I have several reasons for defying my doctors in coming here:

In 2009, CHED gave to Lyceum the highest award for a university — the award of autonomous status;

In 2012, the Philippine Association of Colleges and Universities cited Lyceum for the highest number of accredited programs in this region, and the second highest in the entire country;

And most important of all — Lyceum Batangas rivals Metro Manila universities in terms of population — 9,000 students, who will be voters in the 2016 presidential and senatorial elections.

Hence, I have come in recognition of the fact that some of you will become senators like my good friend and mentor, Dr. Sotero H. Laurel. And at least one of you, I predict, like President Jose P. Laurel, will someday become president of the Philippines.

WHAT IS LEADERSHIP?

Leadership is defined as "a process of social influence in which one person can enlist the aid and support of others in the accomplishment of a common task."

According to authorities, leadership has two

dimensions:

Consideration, which emphasizes good relations. A leader is friendly, approachable, and a good listener.

Initiating structure, which stresses behaviour involved in directing the organization and helping it to define and achieve its goals. This dimension includes the leader's ability to understand the actions others can act upon.

From these two dimensions, we can conclude that a leader performs three basic functions: organizational; interpersonal; and decisional. These functions are essential in the success of a leader. They are played out in the leader's actions and in the leader's relationship with his or her followers.

TRANSACTIONAL V. TRANSFORMATIONAL LEADERSHIP

There are two kinds of leadership: transactional and transformational.

Transactional or managerial leadership is a leadership style that promotes compliance with existing organizational norms through supervision and monitored group performance using traditional rewards and punishments. Transactional leadership is an effective strategy for projects that must closely follow standards to succeed. Transactional leaders are also especially effective in times of crisis, such as the supertyphoon Yolanda.

Transactional leadership can be very effective in the right settings. Good coaches of sports teams are transactional leaders. Sports teams operate within rules with very little flexibility, and adherence to organizational norms is the key to their success. Good coaches are able to motivate their team members to play and win.

Transformational leadership focuses on the followers' morale and engagement, and attempts to link the followers' sense of self with organizational values. This leadership style stresses leading by example. This is the kind of leader whom we should elect in 2016. I call on the legendary courage of the Batangueños to reject any leader involved in the P10 billion pork barrel scandal, and to reelect senators who are fighting to uphold justice among the suspects, despite efforts at black propaganda by the mastermind in the Senate of the plunder conspiracy.

We do not have to choose between these two kinds of leadership; instead we should use both of them.

The full range approach of leadership seeks to blend the best aspects of transactional and transformational leadership into one comprehensive approach. In this approach, the leader uses these techniques from transactional leaders: communicates clear expectations of outcomes and rewards; gives rewards and recognition for accomplishments; and actively monitors the followers' progress and provides supportive feedback. At the same time, the leader, in accordance with transformational leadership, makes interpersonal connections with followers; mentors and coaches others; solicits followers' ideas; encourages creativity and individuality; inspires others to perform; and leads by example.

OTHER LEADERSHIP PERSPECTIVES

Aside from transactional and transformational leadership, there are other leadership perspectives, namely, moral leadership, servant leadership, shared leadership, and emotional leadership, among others.

Moral or ethical leadership focuses on how leaders use their social power in the decisions they make, actions they engage in, and ways they influence others. An effective leader influences a subordinate's attitude and values. Thus, a moral leader has moral influence over his or her followers.

Servant leadership is exercised when the leader is destined to work for people and the community. A servant leader looks at what people need and asks how to help people to solve problems.

Shared leadership means that leadership is distributed within a team, and people within that team lead each other.

Emotional leadership is a process that leaders use to influence their followers in a common goal. Leaders in a positive mood can impact their group in a positive way. Charismatic leaders can transmit their emotions and influence followers through "emotional contagion."[1]

DEVELOPING STUDENT LEADERSHIP

You — the youth who will determine the future of the Philippines — should not only get involved, but also each one of you should be a leader. Leadership is not about personality; it's about behaviour—an observable set of skills and abilities. Leaders are not born; it takes practice to develop the qualities of a leader. Here are some ways to be a leader and develop leadership abilities:

Become an officer of the glee club, the debate team, the student government, or your class. Just step up!

Play to your strengths. Get involved in something you are passionate about.

Even when you don't have the lead role, you can still stand out by contributing as a team player. Being a team player is also a valuable leadership skill.

Sign up for more than one activity. You don't

---

1 https://www.boundless.com/management/leadership/other-leadership-perspectives/

have to be president of every organization you join, but it is important to be well rounded. Don't just stick to your comfort zone. Take time to branch out. You might find a hidden talent you never knew you had.

Be involved in the larger community outside your campus. It shows that you care, that you are versatile, and that you want to make a difference.

Good student leaders share the following characteristics:

Integrity. Integrity is the foundation of leadership, and it is especially important for students trying to establish themselves as lifetime leaders. Leaders with integrity are trustworthy, honest, and able to consistently follow-through on their promises.

Compassion for others. A desire to help others succeed and a simple willingness to help others is the most genuine trait of a student leader. Showing you care motivates other students to follow your example.

Initiative. Student leaders step in when help is needed, they offer support to fellow students, and they overcome peer pressure to do what is right. Student leaders are typically self-starters who push themselves to succeed.

Vision. Student leaders need to have a vision and a sense of purpose to accomplish things.

CONCLUSION: THE 2016 ELECTIONS

I have one final word on student leadership. The 2016 presidential elections will be a test of leadership during these dark days, these particular times when government is investigating the P10 billion pork barrel scandal. As potential leaders of our country, you should practice as leaders by advising your respective communities about the pork barrel scandal in relation to the 2016 elections, as follows:

The Supreme Court has declared pork barrel as unconstitutional. But during the time when pork barrel was still a legitimate exercise of the power to reduce poverty, it became a widespread source of corruption from no less than the leaders of our country. I refer to those who are elected senators and representatives. This sordid case of plunder in our political history is evidence that corruption is caused by a top-down process.

Therefore, we should not reelect any senators or congressmen running for reelection in 2016, if they are among those against whom the Ombudsman will file criminal charges for plunder or malversation in the trial court known as the Sandiganbayan. Of course, every person enjoys a presumption of innocence. But when the Ombudsman conducts the preliminary investigation, she goes over voluminous papers and other documents, as well as affidavits executed by eyewitnesses. She has to do this, because under the law, the Ombudsman who is the prosecutor in this case, has to prove what the law calls a prima facie case. The term prima facie is a Latin phrase which means at first sight, or on first appearance, but subject to further evidence or information. Hence, if the Ombudsman files a case against a reelectionist for plunder in the Sandiganbayan, this means that she has in her possession enough evidence to allow the trial court to rule in favor of the government.

While all this investigation is going on, particularly on television when the Blue Ribbon Committee conducts hearings and examines alleged witnesses, you will notice that certain politicians and other members of the high and mighty in society are conspicuous by their silence. Politicians who purposely refrain from participating in the national debate on the pork barrel scandal are politicians who are cowards, because they refuse to take a position for fear of incurring the anger of the guilty ones. This kind of cowardice is anathema to leadership.

Hence, in conclusion, I urge you to go back to your community, and advise your relatives and neighbors to reject politicians who are consistently silent on the pork barrel scandal. Silence means that the particular politician is willing to make friends with anybody, right or wrong, corrupt or honest, as long as the politician can gather votes. This is the mantra of the unprincipled person. In other words, that candidate is an opportunist. He does not act out of conviction, but acts out of what is convenient for himself. This is the test I want you to apply, as the 2016 elections approach. Apply the test of leadership among the candidates.

In my view, leadership is the courage to take risks in defense of a position that is both legal and moral. The politician who tries to become a wise guy by becoming friends to everybody — corrupt or not — is not a leader. That kind of a politician does not deserve to be invited to the Lyceum of the Philippines University.

That kind of politician I abhor at first sight, and that kind of crook I will fight to the death, even if he has all the money and power in our country; and even if he can afford to pay an entire army of corrupt journalists to destroy me, and an entire army of paid assassins to threaten me. I will take my courage from you people — the great, the good, the very brave Batangueños

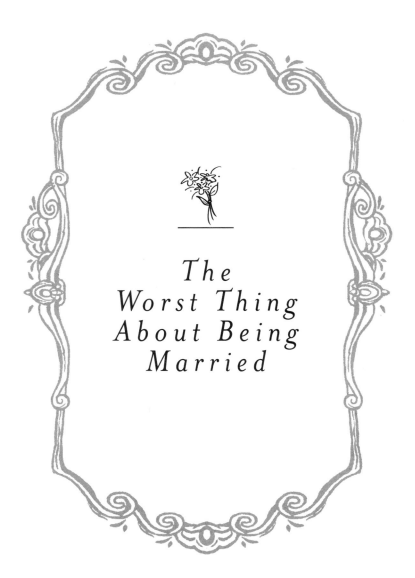

The Worst Thing About Being Married

I think divorce should be available to people who become homicidal at the sight of each other.

———

A survey was conducted to find out what is the first thing men look at when a beautiful woman passes by. According to single men—
35% said they look at the woman's face;
30% said they look at the woman's breasts;
20% said they look at the woman's buttocks when she walks away;
15% said they look at the woman's legs.
But—
100% of married men said they first look at their wives to check if they are looking at them.

———

Men are like horoscopes, they always tell you what to do and are usually wrong.

———

A smart wife is one who makes sure she spends so much that her husband can't afford another woman.

———

Question: What is the punishment for bigamy?
Answer: Two wives.

It is very important that you should choose the person you will marry and stay with that person. There are many people now who believe in serial love, loving one person after another. I don't think that is good for our mental health. I think we should get it over with. It's like measles, you know. You only get it once in your lifetime and you are immune forever. I am very happy to say that is what happened to me. I am completely immune to any temptation. All men who have passed my life after I got married might as well have been sticks of furniture.

—————

After a hard day's work, it's great to come home and have someone to yell at, at the top of my lungs.

—————

I don't smoke, I don't drink, I don't commit adultery. I only tell lies to my husband.

—————

When I got married, I noticed immediatelythat there seems to be a rivalry between the egos of two people. So, if you just kill your ego, there's no problem. To fight with someone who's going to be with you for the rest of your life is so counterproductive. So I just said to my husband on our honeymoon, "I'll go my way, and you'll go my way."

*If you are in a relationship, stop trying to figure out who
wears the pants between the two of you. Relationships
work best when both of you are not wearing pants.*

There is a recent study that more than 60 percent of married men in Metro Manila are unfaithful to their wives. This is because the remaining 40 percent bring their mistresses to the provinces.

Scientists have discovered a food that diminishes a woman's sex drive by 90 percent. Ang tawag doon ay wedding cake.

Five tips for a happy man's life:

Have a girl to help you at work.
Have a girl to take care of you & love you.
Have a girl who can make you laugh.
Have a girl who spoils you.
Lastly, and most importantly,
Siguraduhin na hindi magkakakilala
ang apat na babaeng iyon.

A couple is lying in bed.
The man says: "Right now, for this Women's Day, I am going to make you the happiest woman in the world!"
The woman says: "Oh dear, I will miss you!"

Marriages are made in heaven. But then
again, so are thunder and lightning.

———

After marriage, husband and wife become two sides of a
coin—they can't face each other but they still stay together.

———

Marriage is when a man and a woman become as one.
The trouble starts when they try to decide which one.

———

Before marriage, a man will lie awake all night
thinking about something she said. After marriage,
he will fall asleep before she finishes talking.

———

They say when a man holds a woman's hand before
marriage, that is love. After marriage, that is self-defense.

———

Marriage is love. Love is blind. Therefore,
marriage is an institution for the blind.

———

Marriage is not a word. It is a sentence—a life sentence.

Husband: Love, may taning na ang buhay ko.
Huling gabi ko na 'to, let's make love.
Wife: Heh, tumigil ka nga! Maaga pa akong
gigising bukas, buti ikaw, hindi na!

———

Husband: Parati na lang tayo nag-
aaway! Maghiwalay na lang tayo!
Wife: Sige, maghati tayo ng mga anak!
Husband: Akin ang mga guwapo at maganda!
Wife: 'Sus! Pinili pa yung hindi kanya!

———

Ano sa Tagalog ang: "Eat All You Can,
don't be shy, feel at home!"
Sagot: "Kain lang kayo ng kain, walanghiya
kayo, pakiramdam nyo bahay nyo to!"

The worst thing about being married is having to tolerate the body noises of your spouse, especially as you both grow older.

Advantage at disadvantage ng may-asawa:

Advantage: 'Pag kailangan mo, nandiyan agad.
Disadvantage: 'Pag ayaw mo na, andiyan pa rin!

———

At a cocktail party, one woman said to another,
"Aren't you wearing your wedding ring on the
wrong finger?" The other woman replied,
"Yes, I am. I married the wrong man."

———

Marriage: a community consisting of a master, a
mistress, and two slaves, making in all, two.

———

When the husband says, "Ako ang tigas sa amin."
He really means: "Ako ang tigas- saing ng kanin,
tigas-sampay ng labada, tigas-sama sa palengke,
at tigas-sundo sa eskwela ng mga bata."

———

When the husband says: "Gagawin ko kahit
ayaw ng Misis ko." He really means, "Gagawin
kong maghugas ng pinggan kung ayaw niya,
gagawin kong maglaba kung ayaw niya."

When the husband says, "Kapag sinabi kong hiwalay, HIWALAY!" He really means, "Hiniwalay ko na ang puti sa de-kolor at baka kumupas ang labada."

When the husband says, "Lahat ng utos ko ay pasigaw." He really means, "Hoy, pakibilisan mo naman iyang kape, please, at giniginaw na ako dito sa labahan!"

Adik sa droga: Payag ka na bang magpakasal sa akin?
Babae: Oo, pero ok lang ba sa iyo
kung meron akong past?
Adik: Ok lang, wala naman akong future eh!

Wife: Ibili mo naman ako ng bagong bra.
Husband: 'Wag ka na mag-bra, maliit
naman boobs mo, eh.
Wife: Eh, bakit ikaw, nagbi-brief?

Husband says: When I'm gone you'll never find another man like me. Wife replied: What makes you think I'd want another man like you?!

Wife: My husband and I have what he calls Olympic sex.
Friend: Wow, you must be having a terrific sex life!
Wife: Not really. It only happens once in 4 years.

———

May isang husband na proud na proud na may anim na
anak silang mag-asawa. Sobrang proud siya na ang laging tawag niya sa wife niya ay "Mother of Six." Pero nai-
inis ang wife niya tuwing sasabihin ito ng husband niya.
Nang minsan pagkatapos nilang kumain sa isang
mataong restaurant, malakas na sinabi ng husband
sa wife niya, "Umuwi na tayo, Mother of Six!"
Sumagot din nang malakas ang wife,
"Sige, tayo na, Father of Four!"

*Kapag sinabi sa iyo ng boyfriend mo na nanlalamig na siya
sa iyo, buhusan mo ng gasolina at silaban mo.*

Miriam
on
Miriam

My management style? Spiritual fortitude, intellectual scholarship, and, (smiling) if all else fails, physical violence might prove salutary.
(After winning the Magsaysay Award for government service.)

They were not only rebellious, they were malicious to boot. Naturally I got mad, but I restrained myself. No, I did not throw a chair at my employees. (Laughing) The accurate statement is that I may have rearranged the furniture.
(After scolding a few government employees who declared their intention to have her removed as Immigration Commissioner.)

I'm very results-oriented, and I do have a kamikaze attitude. I don't care if I go down in flames, as long as my enemies and I go down in flames together. Or maybe you can call it the Samson-in-the-temple syndrome. I don't care if I destroy myself, as long as I destroy the temple of corruption. That would be a definite service to the community, don't you think?
(In a magazine cover story.)

I'm surprised the photographer used that shot. He and I had an agreement that he would take shots of me swimming in the pool. I followed all his instructions, exactly as if I were a trained dolphin.
(Explaining the publication in a major newspaper of her controversial photo in a bathing suit.)

———

Nandiyan na 'yan, kasama sa trabaho. Siguro mabuti na ngang lumabas 'yung litratong yon, dahil diyan mapapatunayan na pag sinabi ko ang vital statistics ko, totoo! Patunay na hindi ako sinungaling, hindi kamukha ng mga kalaban ko!
(Laughing at the same photo.)

———

I always put myself in harm's way because that is where I am most effective.

———

Every Filipino dreams in his heart of doing a great, magnificent selfless act of sacrifice for the country. In my case, I tried for President and I failed. Maybe, my best service to the country would be if one working day I strap myself with grenades and just hurl myself bodily onto the center of the Senate Session Hall.

My favorite poetess is Emily Dickinson. She
was a recluse. I'd love to be a recluse , but I
have to be famous before I become a recluse.
Otherwise, I'd simply be called Anonymous.

———

Public opinion is untrustworthy. It is also merciless,
pitiless. I am never allowed to have an off day. When
I speak, I must always be brilliant. I can never have a
day when I can sound dumb like everybody else.

———

Excuse me, I'm not a blushing bride. I'm a veteran wife.

———

Allow me to introduce myself. I am the UP graduate
who has, in a modest way, focused national attention
on the political malady known as logopaedics,
the branch of medicine that deals with speech
disabilities and their treatment. Kasi ang ibang tao
sa impeachment trial, hindi marunong magsabi ng
totoo, kaya binibigyan ko sila ng speech therapy.
(*Commencement speech before the U.P. College of Medicine graduates
on 20 May 2012 at the U.P. Theater in Diliman campus.*)

As the author of the Reproductive Health bill in the Senate, I am preparing my battle gear. After the SONA, we will be ready for a shootout. I am preparing my Navy Seals and my stealth bombers so that we can rescue the people who are suffering from fortress mentality.

I went to see a pulmonologist and then she said, "I'm sorry but you have cancer," and I said, "Yes!" because I wanted a challenge in my life.

If I do not die of cancer, or if I do not die from the medication, I will die from making a living, because these cancer pills are so expensive.

I feel like I am going, going, and soon be gone. Just call me the disappearing senator.
(Miriam on her cancer illness.)

Yes, I am intellectually arrogant. All intellectuals are entitled to be arrogant. That's the only way they can educate the non-intellectual. Inggit lang sila.

"People would be SURPRISED to find out I don't SCREAM" Everyday

I'd normally sit in front where I worship my professor.
I'd stare with lovestruck eyes, take down everything he says
and I don't even breathe. That's how I got to be a scholar
because all my professors knew that I adored them.
(Miriam recounting her student days.)

———

People would be surprised to find
out I don't scream every day.
I resort to this mischievous way of thinking maybe
to relax the neurons in my brain, especially when I
fight with someone with no neurons whatsoever.

———

Walk around naked in Metro Manila. I would
walk around naked and display myself to the
general public and say, "Are you happy now?"
*(Answer to the question: If there were no rules in your life for
one day and you could be outrageous, what would you do?)*

———

Hindi naman ako mataba eh. In fact,
I'm so sexy that it overflows.

Wala naman talagang pangit, sadyang
nasobrahan lang ako sa ganda.

———

Kakatanggap ko lang ng aking medical results. May
sakit daw ako. Habang tumatanda ako, gumaganda
daw ako. Don't worry, hindi ito nakakahawa.
Iyon nga lang, hindi na daw ako gagaling.

———

I never wanted to be a warrior. I wanted to be a scholar.
I consider every act of evil a personal challenge.

I call this dish…"Il Pobre Senadores Ala Utac"

DREAMS TO LIVE FOR

By

Senator Miriam Defensor Santiago

(Commencement speaker at the Lyceum of the Philippines–Laguna

on 24 April 2014)

LESSONS OF LIFE

Nothing matters more to the future of this nation than to ensure that our young women and men learn to believe in themselves and to believe in their dreams. I believe one of our country's most priceless assets is the idealism of our young people. My generation has invested all that it has — not only its love, but also its hope and faith — in your generation.

Hence, allow me to share with you what life has taught me, and in the end to encapsulate for you the meaning of life. First, life teaches us that, whether we perceive it as predestined or random, it is beyond any person's control. Human beings have inhabited this planet for only 250,000 years or .0015 per cent of the history of life, the last inch of the cosmic mile. The earth worked perfectly well without us for billions of years, and it will continue to do so even when we are gone. This fact makes our existence seem more like a happy accident than a carefully thought-out plan.

The second important lesson that life has taught me is this: there is no template for the meaning of life. Instead, the meaning of life is what you choose to make it mean. Life is the consequence of our moral choices.

A MEANINGFUL LIFE

While there is no blueprint for the meaning of life, there is countless research on ways to have a more meaningful life. There are three ways to make your life more meaningful:

First, get connected. While a busy social life with lots of friends may help keep you happy, it is the deeper relationships with loved ones that will truly add meaning to your life.

Second, do not shy away from stress. The things that add the most meaning to our lives — a high-pressure job or caring for a loved one — are often the same things that add the most stress to our day-to-day existence. However, taking the easy road is not always the better option. The biggest challenges in life often lead to the biggest gains in the long run.

Third, find a sense of purpose. Studies show that people who spend more time pursuing activities that reflected their sense of self were the people who found their lives more meaningful. A life filled with meaning is linked to doing things that express and reflect the self.

PREPARING FOR ASEAN INTEGRATION

Your school authorities have requested me to talk on ASEAN integration. Integration means that as a rule, every ASEAN country will treat people and products from any country in the whole ASEAN region, as if they are the people and products coming from the country itself. Thus, integration will mean that in ASEAN among ourselves we will pay less taxes, less customs duties, and less import taxes. The ASEAN countries will form the equivalent of what used to be called the

European Common Market, and what is now called the European Union. All separate neighbors will become bound together into one whole called ASEAN Common Market, with each country entitled to equal participation and membership.

In 2003, the ten member-states of the Association of Southeast Asian Nations (ASEAN) – the Philippines, Brunei, Cambodia, Indonesia, Laos, Malaysia, Myanmar, Singapore, Thailand, and Vietnam – agreed to integrate their economies. In 2007, the leaders of the ASEAN countries approved a "blueprint" to guide each member on initiatives and measures to achieve regional integration which is scheduled for 2015.

ASEAN integration will allow the ten countries and over half a billion people to participate in the free flow of goods, services, labor, capital, and foreign investment. Ultimately, integration will foster greater cooperation and healthy competition in the region.

There are many advantages of ASEAN integration. One advantage is the opening up of job markets in the region. While many Filipinos already work in other ASEAN countries, the process of looking for jobs abroad will be made easier by the integration. But this also means that the job market will be fiercer. Filipinos will have to compete against applicants from other ASEAN nations. However, we have an advantage because we are highly adaptable. We can easily adapt to multicultural workplaces. Our command of the English language is also an advantage over our ASEAN counterparts.

Another advantage is the regional community approach to integration of education in the region. The K-to-12 program has been instituted to make Philippine education comparable to the ASEAN and the rest of the world. The academic calendar synchronization of ASEAN universities lays the groundwork for increasing student and faculty mobility within the region. Only the Philippines starts its academic calendar in June. Most universities in China, Korea, Japan, and North America start their classes in August or September.

This integration is the main reason why some Philippine universities have synchronized their school calendars in 2014 with those of their counterparts in other ASEAN countries. The synchronization of the academic calendar of Philippine universities with most ASEAN, European, and American academic partners will create more joint programs and partnerships with other universities and allow students to get transfer credits from different universities in the ASEAN.

LPU Laguna is ahead of the curve with respect to the ASEAN integration. You have the following desirable assets: experienced educators and mentors; internationally responsive academic programs; and a beautiful and world-class campus conducive to learning. All these make you extremely attractive to foreign students and scholars.

CONCLUSION

In conclusion, allow me to recite some stanzas
from the poem "What I Live For:"

I live for those who love me,
Whose hearts are kind and true;
For the Heaven that smiles above me,
And awaits my spirit too;
For all human ties that bind me,
For the task by God assigned me,
For the bright hopes yet to find me,
And the good that I can do.

I live to hail that season
By gifted ones foretold,
When men shall live by reason,
And not alone by gold;
When man to man united,
And every wrong thing righted,
The whole world shall be lighted
As Eden was of old.

I live for those who love me,
For those who know me true,
For the Heaven that smiles above me,
And awaits my spirit too;
For the cause that lacks assistance,
For the wrong that needs resistance,
For the future in the distance,
And the good that I can do.

1 Stephen Jay Gould on the meaning of life. *http://www. brainpickings.org/index.php/2012/09/17/the-meaning-of-life/*
2 *http://news.health.com/2014/01/22/5-ways-to-have-a-more-meaningful-life/*
3 "Is the Philippines Ready for ASEAN Economic Integration in 2015?", Business Journal, American Chamber of Commerce of the Philippines, Inc., October 2013.

Photo by Menchit Ongpin

MIRIAM DEFENSOR SANTIAGO
Resume
August 2014

GLOBAL FAME

She earned the degree, Doctor of Juridical Science, in the United States. Dr. Miriam Defensor Santiago is a globally famous personality, because of her legal brilliance and courageous example in fighting corruption. In a nation where many public officials are charged with, or suspected, of plunder, her honesty shines like a light in the darkness.

She has brought honor to the Philippines in several ways. She is the first Filipino and the first Asian from a developing country, to be elected in the United Nations as judge of the International Criminal Court. The ICC hears cases against heads of state. Thus, she put the Philippines on the global map in the 21st century. Unfortunately, grave illness forced her to waive the privilege of being an ICC judge.

For two years, she suffered from chronic fatigue syndrome. In June 2014 she was diagnosed with lung cancer, stage 4 (the last stage). But with her signature humor and bravery, she fought back, and her cancer has regressed. Even cancer cells are afraid of her!

She was chosen as laureate of the Magsaysay Award for Government Service, known as the Asian equivalent of the Nobel Prize. She was cited "for bold and moral leadership in cleaning up a graft-ridden government agency." She was named one of "The 100 Most Powerful Women in the World" by The Australian magazine.

ACADEMIC EXCELLENCE

Dr. Santiago is one of the most intellectually brilliant leaders that our country has ever seen. She earned the degrees Bachelor of Arts, magna cum laude; and Bachelor of Laws, cum laude, from the University of the Philippines. She went abroad and earned the graduate degrees of Master of Laws, and Doctor of Juridical Science, from the University of Michigan, one of the top three law schools in the United States. She finished the academic requirements for the degree Master of Arts in Religious Studies, at the Maryhill School of Theology.

In U.P., the perfect grade is 1.0. In her last undergraduate semester, Dr. Santiago earned the near-perfect average grade of 1.1. And she finished her 4-year course in only 3-1/2 years. At the University of Michigan, she was a Barbour Scholar and DeWitt Fellow. She finished her master's degree in only one year, and her doctorate in only six months.

Our guest speaker loves learning. She has done postdoctoral studies all over the world, including Oxford University, Cambridge University, Harvard University, University of California at Berkeley, Stanford University, and Academy of Public International Law at the Peace

Palace (the seat of the International Court of Justice), at The Hague, Netherlands.

Dr. Santiago was class valedictorian at all levels — elementary, high school, and college. She made history in U.P. when she became the first female editor-in-chief of the famous student newspaper, Philippine Collegian, thus shattering a 50-year old record of male dominance. She won as Best Debater in the annual U.P. law debate, where she was captain of the winning team. It is interesting that at the same time she held a campus beauty title, not once but twice — as ROTC corps sponsor.

PROFESSIONAL EXCELLENCE

Dr. Santiago holds an amazing record of excellence in all three branches of government — judicial, executive, and legislative. In the judicial branch, she has been presiding judge of the Regional Trial Court at Quezon City. In the executive branch, she has been immigration commissioner; and a cabinet member, as agrarian reform secretary. In the legislative branch, she has now been a senator for three terms.

Dr. Santiago worked abroad. She served as legal officer of the United Nations in Geneva, Switzerland. She also served as a consultant of the Philippine embassy in Washington, D.C.

In all three branches of government, she has been showered with awards for being outstanding, making her the most awarded public official in our country today. For example, she has received awards such as The Outstanding Young Men, or TOYM; The Outstanding Women in the Nation's Service, or TOWNS; and Most Outstanding Alumna in Law from U.P.

Dr. Santiago was a U.P. law professor for some 10 years, teaching evening class after office hours. She has written some 30 books, many of which are very scholarly textbooks in law and the social sciences, well advanced of our time. During her initial battle with cancer, she continued to work on the 2014 edition of all her law books. She is considered the leading expert of her generation in constitutional law and in international law.

In the Philippine Senate where Dr. Santiago is on her third term, she has filed the highest number of bills, and authored some of the most important laws. Some of her most important pending bills are: anti-dynasty bill; an act institutionalizing an age-appropriate curriculum to prevent the abduction, exploitation, and sexual abuse of children; anti-epal bill; freedom of information bill; and magna carta for Philippine internet freedom. She has been fearless in exposing and naming notorious criminal suspects in legislative investigations, particularly in naming jueteng lords and illegal logging lords.

UNQUESTIONED HONESTY

It was Senator Santiago who in effect started the national plunder investigation (which is now a historic scandal). In December 2012 she revealed that the senate president had used Senate funds to give away cash gifts. Every senator received P2 million as a Christmas gift, taken from public funds, except Senator Santiago and two others. That scandal led to the notorious pork barrel scandal, for which the senate president is now suspended and in jail, having been charged with plunder by the Ombudsman.

COA records show that her "pork barrel," also known as PDAF, was never marred by any kickback, unlike those of her colleagues in Congress. In three separate cases, the Supreme Court had upheld the pork barrel system as constitutional. Sen. Santiago gave her PDAF to: the University of the Philippines system; Philippine General Hospital; and local government units. She never released her pork barrel to any NGO, particularly those headed by those guilty of plunder, which means wholesale stealing of public money by accepting kickbacks, or simply pocketing the entire money.

After the impeachment of the Chief Justice in 2012, it was later revealed that Miriam was one of only three senators who refused to receive the DAP, amounting to P50 million for every senator and P10 million for every congressman. It was also later revealed that three senators even received P100 million each, after the impeachment.

When she was a student in U.P. law school, one magazine dubbed her "Supergirl at the State University." She is probably the public official whose face has graced the highest number of magazine covers. She has been featured by famous international publications, including Time, the New York Times, and the Herald-Tribune.

In 1992, the foreign press reported that she had been elected as President of the Philippines after a nationwide election. However, she was cheated. As the Filipinos say: "Miriam won in the voting, but lost in the counting."

She is a renowned celebrity. Like a rock star, she attracts crowds everywhere. She is the most sought-after guest speaker of university students. Sen. Santiago is a woman of destiny. She will be remembered in Philippine history as a genuine hero of her people.

She has been called the incorruptible lady, the platinum lady, the tiger lady, the dragon lady, the iron lady of Asia, the queen of popularity polls, and the undisputed campus hero. But to her millions of fans, she is best known for the unique brand of charismatic leadership that media likes to call "Miriam Magic."

ILLUSTRATORS

Manix Abrera, *pp 49, 75*

Kay Aranzanso, *p 57*

Jose Noel Avendaño, *p 116*

Rob Cham, *pp 7, 15*

Dark Chapel, *pp 11, 19, 105*

Rommel Estanislao, *pp 61, 79*

Francis Martelino, *pp 71, 81, 97, 106*

Josel Nicolas, *pp 53, 65*

Cj de Silva-Ong, *pp 22, 113*

Elbert Or, *pp 33, 37*

Joshua Panelo, *pp 29, 38*

Julius Villanueva, *p 101*